STEM *trailblazer* BIOS

GOOGLE CYBERSECURITY EXPERT
PARISA TABRIZ

DOMENICA DI PIAZZA

Lerner Publications ◆ Minneapolis

For my father, my favorite explorer and a white hat who is game for so many things

Lerner Publications Company
A division of Lerner Publishing Group, Inc.
241 First Avenue North
Minneapolis, MN 55401 USA

For reading levels and more information, look up this title at www.lernerbooks.com.

Content consultant: Ashley Podhradsky, associate professor of digital forensics and information assurance, Dakota State University

Library of Congress Cataloging-in-Publication Data

Names: Di Piazza, Domenica, author.
Title: Google cybersecurity expert Parisa Tabriz / Domenica Di Piazza.
Description: Minneapolis : Lerner Publications, [2017] | Series: STEM
    trailblazer bios | Audience: Ageg 7-11. | Audience: Grade 4 to 6. |
    Includes bibliographical references and index.
Identifiers: LCCN 2017024974 (print) | LCCN 2017019798 (ebook) | ISBN
    9781541500082 (eb pdf) | ISBN 9781541500075 (lb : alk. paper) | ISBN
    9781541512160 (pb : alk. paper)
Subjects: LCSH: Tabriz, Parisa—Juvenile literature. | Google
    (Firm)—Biography—Juvenile literature. | Computer
    programmers—Biography—Juvenile literature. | Computer networks—Security
    measures—Juvenile literature. | Computer crimes—Prevention—Juvenile
    literature.
Classification: LCC HD8039.D37 (print) | LCC HD8039.D37 D57 2017 (ebook) |
    DDC 005.8/092 [B] —dc23
LC record available at https://lccn.loc.gov/2017024974

Manufactured in the United States of America
1-43643-33460-6/21/2017

The images in this book are used with the permission of: courtesy of Everett Collection, p. 4;
© Rob Latour/Variety/REX/Shutterstock, p. 5; courtesy of Parisa Tabriz, pp. 7, 8, 9 (photo by Brandon Downey), 16 (photo by meder); 18, 22, 26 (photo by Bryan William Jones), 27 (photo by Patrick Nehls), 28; © Feng Cheng/Dreamstime.com, p. 10; AP Photo/Dave Pickoff, p. 12; iStock.com/g-stockstudio, p. 14; Kim Kulish/Corbis/Getty Images, p. 15; courtesy of Google, pp. 17, 20, 21; John D. Johnson, p. 23; Ann Hermes/The Christian Science Monitor/Getty Images, p. 24: iStock.com/maciek905, p. 25.

Cover: © Rob Latour/Variety/REX/Shutterstock.

Main body text set in Adrianna Regular 13/22. Typeface provided by Chank.

CONTENTS

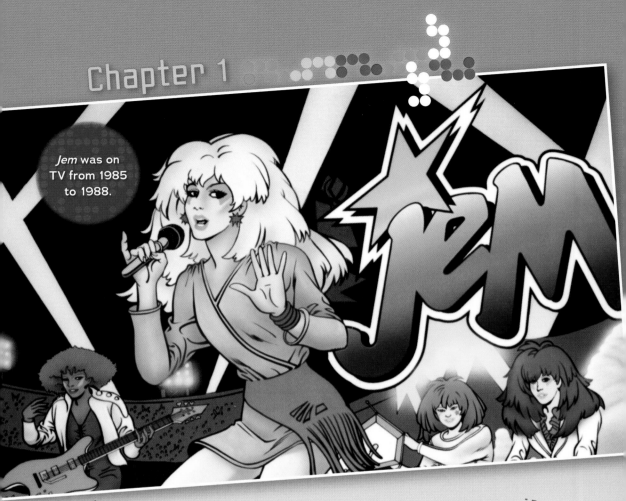

Chapter 1

Jem was on TV from 1985 to 1988.

PLAYING THEM AT THEIR OWN GAME

When she was a little girl, Parisa Tabriz wanted to be like the title character in the 1980s TV show *Jem*. Jem is the lead singer of a rock band called Jem and the Holograms. She has a secret identity. She's really a shy girl named Jerrica

Benton. Jerrica uses her father's computer to make an alternate 3-D version of herself—a pink-haired rocker!

As an adult, Tabriz is not a musical rock star. And she doesn't have a 3-D version of herself. But like Jem, she thinks outside the box to come up with creative ideas. That skill makes her great at what she does.

Tabriz needs to think in creative ways to do her job.

Tabriz is a rock-star **hacker** for the technology company Google. She is a white hat, or a computer security expert who makes sure information on the Internet is safe. White hats spend a lot of time looking for **bugs** (errors and weaknesses) in software. They actually try to hack (break into) their own software so they can fix the bugs. By writing better software, white hats make sure bad-guy hackers—the black hats—can't steal passwords, credit card numbers, or private messages. Tabriz loves the creative people she works with. She loves thinking like the bad guys so she and her team can figure out how to protect computer users.

GOOGLE

Google founders Larry Page and Sergey Brin met as students at Stanford University in California. The company's name is based on *googol*. This math term stands for the numeral 1 followed by 100 zeros. Page and Brin wanted to help people find huge amounts of information on the web. They succeeded, and Google became the most popular search engine in the world.

IMMIGRANT DAUGHTER

Parisa Tabriz was born in 1983. She grew up in a suburb of Chicago, Illinois. Her father, Rahim Tabriz, is a doctor. He came to the United States from Iran. Tabriz's mother, Valerie Tabriz, is Polish American. She is a nurse. Tabriz has two younger brothers, David and Michael.

As kids, Tabriz and her brothers were very competitive. They loved sports and video games—and they played to win. Tabriz says she learned to use her mind to compete with her brothers. "When I couldn't outmuscle them, I had to outthink them," she recalls.

Tabriz (*bottom*) still has close relationships with her family.

Tabriz didn't know what kind of work she wanted to do. Maybe she would be an artist since she loved to draw and paint. In high school, she was good at math and science. She took a career test to find out how she could use her strengths and interests. The test said she would be a good police officer. Tabriz later said the test wasn't wrong. As a security expert at Google, her job is to protect people—just like police officers do.

Chapter 2

The University of Illinois at Urbana-Champaign (UIUC) campus

INSPIRATION

Tabriz went to college in 2001 at the University of Illinois at Urbana-Champaign (UIUC). Because she was good at math and science, she planned to study engineering, the science of designing machines and structures. At college, she taught herself to build websites. It was a way to be artistic. Tabriz used a free online service to build the sites.

She didn't like the ads the service put on her sites. So she hacked the service to remove the ads. She loved figuring out how to trick the service so she could be in charge. That's how she decided to study computer science. Luckily, UIUC has one of the world's best computer science programs.

Tabriz joined a computer security club at UIUC. She got together with other students on Friday nights in the basement of the computer science building. Tabriz was the only woman.

Members of the club knew a lot about computer security, but they didn't know how to hack using the Internet. Tabriz showed them what she knew. She taught them cross-site scripting (XSS). She also taught them cross-site request forgery (XSRF). XSS and XSRF are easy ways for hackers to trick websites and browsers by sending them new instructions. The instructions can cause a website to reveal private information stored there or harm the website.

TECH TALK

"There were no university classes in security [when I was in school]. Everything [our college computer club] knew, we learned from each other."

—Parisa Tabriz

GETTING INSIDE THE MINDS OF THE BAD GUYS

In the summer of 2005, Tabriz interned at Sandia National Laboratories in Livermore, California. The lab studies new technology such as clean forms of energy. There, she developed tools to improve cybersecurity.

John Draper is an infamous hacker who went to prison multiple times for illegal hacking activities.

She had another internship the next summer at Google, in Mountain View, California. She was a security intern and learned more about tools to combat black hats. In 2006, she earned her master's degree from UIUC. Her internship and degree led to a full-time job at Google. She started in 2007 as an information security engineer. She worked with a team of ten people. The team was in charge of software security.

CAPTAIN CRUNCH

During college, Tabriz heard about a hacker known as Captain Crunch. His real name is John Draper. In the 1960s, long-distance calls were expensive. Draper discovered how to make free long-distance calls.

Draper used a small whistle that came in boxes of Cap'n Crunch cereal. The whistle made the same noise the phone company AT&T used to route international phone calls. Draper was arrested for phone fraud in 1972. His story helped Tabriz realize that there are many ways to hack a system.

The team's job was to get inside the minds of black hats. Black hats steal personal information. They want passwords, account numbers, and answers to security questions. They use that information to break into accounts to steal money. Or they sneak onto a computer system and trick or force users to download harmful software.

Black hats look for weak spots in computer systems that they can use to access private information.

Larry Page (*left*) and Sergey Brin started Google in 1998.

The biggest hack against Google users so far began in late 2016. Harmful software called **malware** infected as many as 1.3 million cell phones. The malware steals Google account information. It forces users into downloading ads. Each download and each click on an ad makes money for the hackers. They earn as much as $320,000 a month. Tabriz and her team are working hard to stop such attacks.

Chapter 3

Tabriz climbs outside and at climbing walls indoors.

GOOGLE'S SELF-DESCRIBED
SECURITY PRINCESS

Tabriz starts each day with rock climbing. She says the activity is like looking for a bug in one of Google's products. "There are no rules," she says. "There is no hard and fast way of doing it."

At Google, Tabriz worked to protect the company's software. She was good at her job. She was promoted in 2011 and became an information security engineering manager. Soon she was promoted again. She was the Chrome security engineering manager. Chrome is Google's **web browser**.

TOP SECRET WEAPON

Tabriz manages 30 of the 250 people on the Google Chrome team. They look for errors in the mountains of computer code that drive the browser. They hunt for bugs in laptops and desktops that run Chrome. They search for bugs in the software that runs Chrome.

Google has a huge campus in Mountain View.

Chrome also has a website for reporting bugs. Google offers cash to outside hackers who find bugs in Chrome products. Google will pay from $500 to $100,000! Then Tabriz's team works to fix the problems people report on the website. Sometimes the team finds bugs on Internet sites that Chrome users visit. So the team creates warnings for users. One warning is a red triangle with an exclamation point. It means black hats may be stealing information from the site. The team also lets users know when a site is secure. Chrome's symbol for a safe site is a green padlock.

Tabriz makes sure to relax outside of work. One of her hobbies is making gelato, a kind of ice cream.

SCRAMBLED MESSAGES

Tabriz knows all about **encryption**. This is a way to write code to scramble messages to make them unreadable. When a website scrambles information, only users with the proper passwords can read it. Black hats can't—unless they discover the key to figure out the code.

You can tell if a website is safe by its address. Web addresses beginning with https are usually safe. The *s* stands for "secure." It means the site is sending and receiving encrypted information.

RESIDENT HACKERS

Tabriz also trains coworkers. She shows engineers how to prevent bugs in the code they write. She teaches the engineers how to think like a hacker. Once she asked engineers to hack a vending machine that sells chocolate. One student put a foreign coin worth less than the cost of the chocolate into the machine. It worked!

NAP PODS

Google is a fun place to work. Employees may have meetings on seven-person bicycles. Tabriz sometimes works in a café on Google's campus. Other people work on laptops in a small pool filled with colorful balls. The company also has nap pods, where people can take a short power nap. They wake up refreshed and ready to get back to creative work.

Some people at Google have fun job titles. Tabriz thought "information security engineer" was boring. So she calls herself Security Princess. And that's what her business cards say!

Google employees aren't always at their desks. The campus is full of cozy places to work.

Workers are encouraged to have fun and build strong relationships with one another at Google.

TECH TALK

"It's important that . . . people feel that they're part of [Google], and that the company is like a family to them. When you treat people that way, you get better productivity."

—*Larry Page*

Chapter 4

Tabriz loves her job. She wants to get more women involved with computer science.

HACKING FOR GOOD

Most of the people Tabriz works with are men. She says, "We . . . need to be reaching out to younger women and girls by providing scholarships and mentoring [them] about getting involved in STEM."

Tabriz is helping get women involved. She goes to r00tz Asylum in Las Vegas, Nevada. At this convention, kids learn to be white hats. They learn to hack for good, not evil. One of the moms who attended r00tz says that she wants her daughters to be exposed to smart women like Tabriz who work in technology.

At r00tz Asylum, presenters teach kids hacking skills. Presenters encourage kids to use their skills to create a better world.

P@$$w0rds

Rank	Password
1	123456
2	password
3	12345678
4	qwerty
5	abc123
6	123456789
7	111111
8	1234567
9	iloveyou
10	adobe123

Tabriz asks the kids questions about computer science. She gives them blinking yo-yos when they answer. She also uses games to teach encryption. An easy game teaches kids the Julius Caesar cipher. In this encryption technique, each letter of the alphabet is replaced with another letter. For example, *BROWN FOX* might be *YOLTK CLU.*

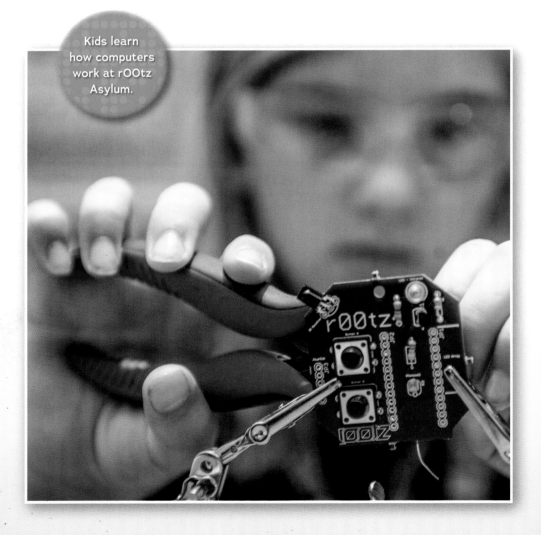

Kids learn how computers work at r00tz Asylum.

READY, SET, GO!

Tabriz has tips for a career in cybersecurity. She says to learn how computers and software work. Learn to write code—and how to break it! And take psychology classes to learn how people think.

Tabriz says it's important to do things, not just read about them. Join a club. Go to a convention. Share what you know. And learn how to explain things so others understand.

Tabriz says the fight against black hats will never end. People are always coming up with new ways to hack computers—and new ways to stop them!

If you work in cybersecurity, you will sometimes fail. Black hats can be just as smart as white hats. So Tabriz says to ask for help when you need it.

LOOKING FORWARD

Tabriz and others are working on new security technologies. She says one day we will not use passwords to access accounts and devices. Our fingerprints will identify us instead, as they already do on many devices. And more of our everyday items will have smart chips. The chips store data. They protect privacy so only you can use your credit card, driver's license, or phone card.

Tabriz says security is a lot better than it used to be. Experts don't always get things right. But when they do, she says, "We can do some pretty impressive stuff."

Tabriz (*front row, center*) posed for this photo with some members of the Google Chrome security team.

"The coolest thing about my job . . . is that I get to work with some of the most passionate and brilliant people in the world to make software that betters people's lives."

—*Parisa Tabriz*

Tabriz likes to have bold adventures when she's away from her computer.

TIMELINE

1983

Parisa Tabriz is born in Chicago, Illinois.

2001

Tabriz begins college at the University of Illinois Urbana-Champaign.

2006

Tabriz earns her master of science degree in computer science.

2007

Tabriz becomes an information security engineer at Google in California.

2011

Tabriz is promoted to information security engineering manager at Google. In less than a year, she is promoted to Chrome security engineering manager.

2012

Forbes magazine names Tabriz one of thirty top experts under the age of thirty to keep an eye on in the field of technology.

2015

Tabriz marries neuroscientist Emerson Stewart.

2017

Tabriz cochairs the Enigma security and privacy conference in Oakland, California.

SOURCE NOTES

8   Clare Malone, "Meet Google's Security Princess," *Elle*, July 8, 2014, http://www.elle
.com/culture/tech/a14652/google-parisa-tabriz-profile.

11 Christine Ryan, "Hot 20: Google's Security Princess, Parisa Tabriz," *7x7*, October 16,
2013, http://www.7x7.com/hot-20-googles-security-princess-parisa
-tabriz-1786549198.html.

16 Cade Metz, "With Any Luck, This Googler Will Turn More Girls into Hackers," *Wired*,
August 26, 2014, https://www.wired.com/2014/08/with-any-luck-this-googler-will
-turn-more-girls-into-hackers.

21 Adam Lashinsky, "Larry Page: Google Should Be Like a Family," *Fortune*, January 19,
2012, http://fortune.com/2012/01/19/larry-page-google-should-be-like-a-family.

22 Alex Jackson, "Google Chrome's Security Lead on STEM, Women in Technology and
Fighting Cyber Crime," *Soapbox Science* (blog), February 20, 2014, http://blogs.nature
.com/soapboxscience/2014/02/20/google-chromes-security-lead-on-stem-women
-in-technology-and-fighting-cyber-crime.

25 Ryan, "Hot 20."

27 Parisa Tabriz, "So, You Want to Work in Security?," *FreeCodeCamp*, July 28, 2016,
https://medium.freecodecamp.com/so-you-want-to-work-in-security-bc6c10157d23#
.umza17pdr.

28 Peter Osterlund, "Parisa Tabriz, Google's 'Security Princess,' Talks about College,"
60second Recap, October 10, 2013, http://www.60secondrecap.com/parisa-tabriz
-google-security-princess.

GLOSSARY

bugs
errors or problems in computer
coding that can harm users or
make a program fail

encryption
a way to scramble a message so
that it is unreadable

hacker
a person who knows how to
gain access to and interfere with
information in a computer system

malware
software that damages computers,
makes them fail, or steals
information

web browser
a computer program used to
explore the Internet

FURTHER INFORMATION

BOOKS

Gagne, Tammy. *Women in Computer Science*. Mankato, MN: Abdo, 2017. Computer scientists code programs on computers, tablets, and smartphones. This book introduces women who are making a difference in this field.

Ignotofsky, Rachel. *Women in Science: 50 Fearless Pioneers Who Changed the World*. New York: Ten Speed, 2016. Meet fifty amazing women scientists, including computer scientists Ada Lovelace and Grace Hopper. Enjoy the fabulous illustrations while you're at it.

Lyons, Heather, and Elizabeth Tweedale. *Coding, Bugs, and Fixes*. Minneapolis: Lerner Publications, 2017. Learn how to program computers, what happens when instructions are out of order, and how mistakes are fixed. Once you know the basics, try coding yourself!

WEBSITES

Nova Cybersecurity Lab

http://www.pbs.org/wgbh/nova/labs/lab/cyber
Learn more about online security at this PBS site just for kids. Meet experts in the field. Learn about coding and hacking. Watch videos and play games about cybersecurity.

r00tz Asylum

https://r00tz.org
Learn more about this hacking convention for kids. Read articles and listen to experts talk about cybersecurity, hear from people who have been to the convention, and more.

LERNER

SOURCE

Expand learning beyond the printed book. Download free, complementary educational resources for this book from our website, www.lerneresource.com.

INDEX

ABOUT THE AUTHOR

Domenica Di Piazza is an editorial director in nonfiction publishing. She also writes nonfiction books for young readers. She enjoys travel, Afro fusion dance, and learning about technology. She would love to learn to rock climb, just like Parisa Tabriz. Di Piazza lives in Minneapolis with her spouse and their dog and three cats.